P9-ARY-246

DISCARDED

CARY AREA LIBRARY
CARY, ILLINOIS 60013

NOV 2 0 2000

DEMCO

IN THE MEADOW

David M. Schwartz *is an award-winning author of children's books, on a wide variety of topics, loved by children around the world.* Dwight Kuhn's *scientific expertise and artful eye work together with the camera to capture the awesome wonder of the natural world.*

For a free color catalog describing Gareth Stevens Publishing's list of high-quality books and multimedia programs, call 1-800-542-2595 (USA) or 1-800-461-9120 (Canada). Gareth Stevens Publishing's Fax: (414) 225-0377. See our catalog, too, on the World Wide Web: gsinc.com

Library of Congress Cataloging-in-Publication Data

Schwartz, David M.
    In the meadow / by David M. Schwartz; photographs by Dwight Kuhn.
        p. cm. — (Look once, look again)
    Includes bibliographical references (p. 23) and index.
    Summary: Introduces, in simple text and photographs, the characteristics of
some of the animals and plants that can be found in a meadow. Includes a black-eyed
Susan, spider, fawn, snake, dandelion, grasshopper, and fox.
    ISBN 0-8368-2223-4 (lib. bdg.)
    1. Meadow animals—Juvenile literature. 2. Meadow plants—Juvenile literature.
[1. Meadow animals. 2. Meadow plants.] I. Kuhn, Dwight, ill. II. Title. III. Series:
Schwartz, David M. Look once, look again.
QL115.5.S39   1998
578.74'6—dc21   98-15407

This North American edition first published in 1998 by
Gareth Stevens Publishing
1555 North RiverCenter Drive, Suite 201
Milwaukee, Wisconsin 53212 USA

First published in the United States in 1997 by Creative Teaching Press, Inc., P. O. Box 6017, Cypress, California, 90630-0017.

Text © 1997 by David M. Schwartz; photographs © 1997 by Dwight Kuhn. Additional end matter © 1998 by Gareth Stevens, Inc.

All rights to this edition reserved to Gareth Stevens, Inc. No part of this book may be reproduced, stored in a retrieval system, or transmitted in any form or by any means, electronic, mechanical, photocopying, recording, or otherwise without the prior written permission of the publisher except for the inclusion of brief quotations in an acknowledged review.

Printed in the United States of America

1 2 3 4 5 6 7 8 9 02 01 00 99 98

IN THE MEADOW

by David M. Schwartz

photographs by Dwight Kuhn

A SPRINGBOARDS INTO
SCIENCE
SERIES

Gareth Stevens Publishing
MILWAUKEE

This flower brightens meadows in summer.
Some people think it has a black eye.

The black-eyed Susan's dark center is brown, not black. It looks like a bull's-eye so insects can find it. Insects eat the flower's sweet-smelling nectar.

This flower is also called "brown-eyed Susan," "brown Betty," and "yellow daisy."

You have two eyes and two legs. This creature has *eight* eyes and *eight* legs!

LOOK AGAIN

Some spiders spin webs to trap their prey, but this jumping spider does not spin a web. It hunts in a different way. First, it spots an insect. Then, it pounces on its victim. Finally, it sucks out the insides of its prey.

Spiders do not chew their food. A spider's mouth works like a straw, drawing in food like a milkshake.

Oh dear, oh dear! What has spots all over its coat?

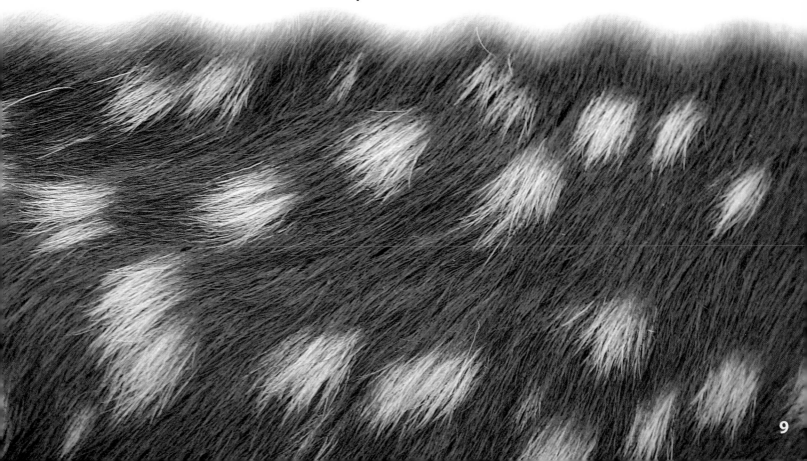

It's a baby deer,
or fawn. Spots
help camouflage the
fawn so it can hide in a
meadow full of flowers. As the
fawn grows, its spots disappear.

Hard, shiny scales help this animal slither away.

It is a smooth green snake. A snake does not have legs. To move, it pushes off the ground with the scales on its belly and slithers away.

These little "parachutes" didn't fall out of a plane. They came from a plant. Blow on them, and they will fly through the air.

They are the seeds of a dandelion. Yellow dandelion flowers become soft, fluffy seed heads. Each seed has its own parachute. When the wind blows, these seed parachutes ride the wind.

No one knows where the seeds will land. They may land in another meadow where they can grow into more dandelions.

This leg is made for hopping — hopping in the grass.

A grasshopper springs into the air with its powerful legs. The back legs have spines that grab onto plants. The grasshopper holds on while it eats a grassy meal.

Some male grasshoppers "sing" by rubbing their wings together to make a loud noise. This is how they attract mates.

What animal has a white tip on its red tail? If you know, you're as clever as a . . .

…fox! The red fox uses its tail for balance when it runs through the meadow. It looks for a red tail with a bright white tip when it wants to find another red fox.

The red fox covers its nose with its tail when it goes to sleep.

A.

B.

C.

D.

E.

F.

G.

Look closely. Can you name these plants and animals?

A.

Black-eyed Susan

B.

Jumping spider

C.

Fawn

D.

Smooth green snake

E.

Dandelion

F.

Grasshopper

G.

Red fox

How many were you able to identify correctly?

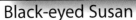

bull's-eye: the small, round area in the center of a target.

camouflage: a way of disguising something or someone to make it look like its surroundings. A camouflaged animal blends in with its habitat.

clever: smart; showing a quick mind.

fawn: a young deer, especially one that is less than a year old.

jumping spider: a type of spider that pounces on its prey instead of catching it in a web like many types of spiders. The spider then sucks out the insides of the prey.

mate (n): the male or female of a pair of animals.

meadow: a grassy area.

nectar: the sweet liquid some flowers make that attracts insects and other animals.

parachute: something that is used to slow the fall of a person or object through the air.

pounces: jumps on quickly, like a spider on its prey.

prey: an animal that is hunted by other animals and some plants for food.

scales: the small, thin, platelike parts that cover a reptile or fish.

slither: to move by sliding and gliding.

spines: sharp points that stick out from some plants and animals. Grasshoppers have spines on their back legs.

Cary Area
1806 Three Oaks
Cary, IL 60013

ACTIVITIES

Magnified Meadow

Little creatures live in the grass of a meadow, even though we may not see them. It can be fun to investigate these animals. With a long piece of string, make a circle on the grass in your backyard or in a park. Use a magnifying glass to hunt for insects and other small animals that might be living within the circle. Draw a picture of those you find. Be sure not to harm them.

Seed Safari

A dandelion seed has a "parachute" to help it float through the air to a different area, where it can grow into a new plant. What other seeds are carried by the wind? Do you know of any "hitchhiker" seeds that travel from place to place on people's clothing or on animals?

Let's Go to the Hop!

Animals that live in a meadow move in many different ways. Snakes slither, grasshoppers hop, and jumping spiders jump. Fold a piece of paper in half the long way. On one side of the paper, make a list of ten kinds of animals that live in the meadow. On the other side, write how each animal moves through the meadow. Then imitate each one!

Make a Meadow Bird Book

At the library, look at a bird book. What kinds of birds live in a meadow? What do they eat? What materials do they use to build their nests? What features help them survive? Make your own meadow bird book by drawing pictures of the birds you have discovered. List their particular features beside the drawings.

More Books to Read

The Deer in the Forest. Linda Gamlin (Gareth Stevens)
Fangs! (series). Eric Ethan (Gareth Stevens)
Grasshoppers. Graham Coleman (Gareth Stevens)
Nature Close-Ups (series). Densey Clyne (Gareth Stevens)
Seeds. Terry J. Jennings (Gloucester Press)
Spotlight on Spiders. Nature Close-Ups (series). Densey Clyne (Gareth Stevens)

Videos

Mother Deer and Her Twins. (Encyclopædia Britannica Educational Corporation)
Snakes. (Rainbow Educational Video)
The Spider. (Barr Films)
What's in Your Backyard? (MBG Videos)

Web Sites

www.adventure.com/encyclopedia/bug/rfigshop.html
dns.ufsia.ac.be/Arachnology/Pages/Kids.html

Some web sites stay current longer than others. For further web sites, use your search engines to locate the following topics: *arachnids, dandelions, deer, flowers, grasshoppers,* and *insects.*

INDEX